Happy Birthday Ellen,

With lots of love,

Ruth

xxx

FREAKSHAKES

Mega milkshakes for sweet tooth fanatics

PAUL CADBY

PAVILION

Contents

Introduction

Born on 4 July, 2014 – well not quite born, conceived perhaps – that's when as a self-confessed foodie exploring the internet, I first started pinning photos of super-indulgent, amazing-looking freakshakes. These crazy creations had found their way to trendy London cafés from their origins in Canberra, Australia, where a café and bakery called Patissez started loading their shakes with all sorts of sweet and savoury treats, sauces and sprinkles. It was then I decided freakshakes would make a great addition to my café in the Cotswolds, so I started work on creating my own versions. My freakshakes had to be temptingly indulgent, an occasional treat, the sort of thing that you don't go near if you're counting calories, as well as fun, funky and frivolous.

I've been at the pointy end of the food and drink industry (customer facing) since I was ten years old, when I first helped out at mum's small hotel. (I even brewed my own beer and sold it to visitors to the Cheltenham races well before I was old enough to drink myself!) Food and drink trends have always fascinated me; I'm drawn to new, different and quirky ideas from all around the world – what's happening, what's not, what's cool and what's hot?

This enthusiasm spurred a summer researching recipes and finding the right premises. Meanwhile, our two dogs, Annie and Lilly, had got very used to having me around and once everything started to line up my wife pointed out that the dogs were going to be proper down in the dumps when I started working full-time again. Well, that's how the Blue Dogs Kitchen was born and named… A year on, with a second café due to open, I'm sharing my recipes and secrets with you. I hope you, your friends and family enjoy them as much as our customers do.

What makes a freakshake?

We start with the glass, the originals use Mason jars, but as our shakes are predominantly made to takeaway we use good-quality disposable glasses. The next step is to brush the inside of the glass with a little ganache, then spread more ganache around the lip using a palette knife – we're not shy with it, this is the "glue" that holds the rim dressing in place and it's not a problem if some of the ganache runs down the inside or the outside of the glass; it all adds to the indulgence.

Now the shake… we start with chilled, good-quality custard (page 10), made using the best vanilla, sugar, cream and free-range egg yolks, and slowly churned to a rich, smooth ice cream. Then we add our flavouring ingredients and blend just long enough to make sure everything is silky smooth, but still super thick – too thin and the toppings will sink.

The shake is poured into the ganache-coated glass, just below the rim (too full and everything overflows), and then topped with a generous serving of freshly whipped double (heavy) cream, flavoured or not.

Next, come the toppings – honeycomb, marshmallows, cookies, brownies, candies and more – as a rule, the more over the top the better the freakshake.

Now for the final flourish, a sweet sauce and maybe a few sprinkles, a straw and a spoon and it's good to go. It's great to hear our customers ooohs and ahhhhhhs as they watch the creation of their freakshake; the theatre is very much part of the fun at Blue Dogs.

And we're done… time for a photo close-up ready to share on social media!

Malting your shake

A malt was originally a fermented health drink, made primarily from the grain of the barley plant, and became big in American soda fountains during the 1920s and 30s, the years of prohibition. Malted milk powder has since become a popular addition to milkshakes. It gives another layer of flavour, a hidden depth and complexity, and also works well in a grown-up creation. Add a spoonful or two of malted milk drink powder to your shake mix for that deep, malty flavour. You may find that it thickens the shake more than normal, but that's no bad thing in a freakshake base.

Boozy, creamy cocktails

There are no strict rules when adding booze to a shake, but moderation is key for various reasons: alcohol doesn't freeze at domestic freezer temperatures and because of this acts as an anti-freeze so your shake won't be as thick as it should be if you overdo it. Adding too much can also cause the alcohol and dairy elements to split, curdling the mixture. Just like a classic cocktail, combine ingredients that complement each other and experiment with flavour.

A few words on equipment

Most of the equipment you need to make a freakshake is standard kitchen kit, so I won't bore you by going into great detail. The key piece of equipment is, of course, a blender but not all blenders are made equal.

At Blue Dogs, having tried expensive commercial blenders we now use bullet-style smoothie blenders. There are lots of different makes and models at many price points… most work, the question is how well and for how long?

If you're blending smoothies and shakes regularly, don't go down the budget route; the more powerful (watts) the motor, the more efficient it will be and the longer it's likely to last. Some models need to be held (with downward pressure) to engage the motor; this isn't an issue occasionally, however if making multiple shakes or regularly blending, it could be restrictive and time consuming – you could be dressing the glass rim while the blender is doing its thing.

Bullet blenders normally come with two different size cups… we find that the larger cup normally gives a faster, smoother blend. Whatever you do don't over fill the cup, the max line is there for a reason, exceed it and you will be putting too much pressure on the motor and seals, causing the cup/blade assembly to wear prematurely and leak. Watch out for the blade, I've often jabbed myself unwittingly.

When blending a lot of ice/frozen products, the blades can dull over time, but you can usually buy replacements from reputable manufacturers. I've tried sharpening the blades with little or no success.

Avoid using a classic milkshake maker – when you're adding ingredients such as fresh/frozen fruit, caramels, fudge or nuts, it will just clog up and throw the contents of the beaker around the room. Messy! Similarly, a food processor, designed for general kitchen duties such as making pastry or cutting vegetables, will beat rather than blend the mixture. It works as a one off or for occasional use – give it a go – but you will need to scrape down the sides to ensure even blending, and because it takes longer than a blender, you will find the ice cream melts more than is ideal.

Other useful bits of kit include disposable piping (pastry) bags, a palette knife for spreading the ganache, thick straws to suck up your shake and lots of napkins to wipe up spills and faces.

How to build a freakshake

Now you know how we construct our freakshakes, the same basic rules apply when you're building your own. Remember this is meant to be fun…

DESIGN
Decide what you want to put into, around and on top of your creation. Choose flavours that complement rather than clash with or overpower the main milkshake. Also, consider colour, texture, shape and variety. Get everything to hand before you start your build, and have the cream whipped and ready to pipe.

GLASSWARE
Anything from a recycled glass jar to a beer or sundae glass goes. Visually, thick glass is better than fine glass, and your creation will also stay cooler for longer, especially if you chill the glass well before starting. Ceramic also keeps the temperature down – you will only see the topping, but it does add to the surprise. How about a seaside bucket and spade set, a goldfish bowl or vase? They all add to the theatre and don't forget freakshakes are great to share – two straws are better than one!

BUILD
Now for the fun bit…

* Add a light smear of ganache to the inside of the glass with a palette knife or the back of a spoon, then add a generous layer around the rim of the glass.

* Stick your rim dressing to the ganache, this helps to contain your shake and forms a slight seal with the cream.

* Blend your shake and pour it into your prepared chilled glass, about 1cm/½in below the rim so the shake doesn't overflow.

* Pipe or spoon whipped cream on top of the shake in the shape of an inverted cone and right to the edge of the glass to stop the shake overflowing. It doesn't need to be perfect as you'll be covering a lot of it.

* Time for the top dressing… working around the glass, start with the longer and larger items, then add the straw and spoon, and fill any gaps with smaller treats; aim for a pyramid or teepee shape as everything will sit and stay in place more easily and for longer without sinking into the shake. Gravity is the enemy of the freakshake, so always be wary of using toppings that are too large or heavy.

* Finish your freakshake with a sweet, sticky sauce and a few sprinkles.

MUST-KNOW RECIPES

Vanilla custard ice cream

**MAKES ABOUT 750ML/
26FL OZ/3 CUPS**

500ml/18fl oz/2 cups double
   (heavy) cream
2 vanilla pods, halved
   lengthways, seeds
   scraped out
70g/2½oz/scant ½ cup
   caster (superfine) sugar
3 free-range egg yolks

**✿ At Blue Dogs, we
try to keep ahead
of ourselves, always
topping up our caster
(superfine) sugar and
rotating the vanilla pod
halves from every batch
of custard, we then
use the older pods that
have already imparted
their flavour into the
sugar when heating the
cream for an extra hit
of vanilla.**

The basis of a great ice cream is a great custard, made using
the best ingredients. This custard takes only 10 minutes to whip
up, but you must let it cool before freezing.

METHOD
Slowly bring the cream and vanilla pods, reserving the seeds, to
the boil in a saucepan, then stir in the sugar until it has dissolved.

Whisk the egg yolks in a large bowl. Continue to whisk while
adding a ladleful of the hot cream mixture to the yolks; this
helps to stop the yolks scrambling. Slowly whisk in the rest of the
hot cream mixture. Return to the pan and heat gently, stirring
continually, until thickened to a custard consistency. Do not let
the mixture boil.

Pour the mixture through a fine sieve (strainer) or muslin
(cheesecloth) into a second bowl and remove the vanilla pods.
(Rinse and save them to make vanilla sugar, see left.) Whisk in
the reserved vanilla seeds and leave to cool.

Pour the mixture into a freezer-proof container and freeze for
2–3 hours or until set. As there is no milk in the ice cream, you
won't need to churn or stir it as ice crystals won't form. You now
have a smooth, indulgent ice cream, and the perfect base for
your freakshake.

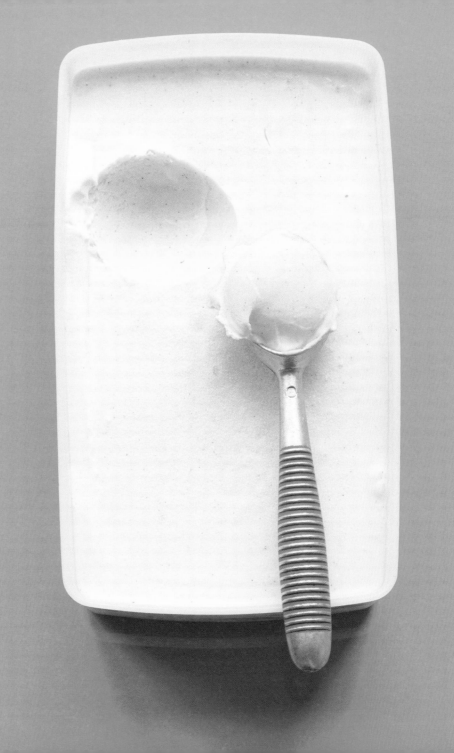

Chocolate ganache

Ganache – white or plain chocolate – has many uses, not only does it play a crucial part in freakshakes. The texture of the ganache needs to be quite thick; it's the "glue" that holds the dressing to the rim of the glass.

MAKES ABOUT 750G/1LB 10OZ

300ml/10fl oz/1¼ cups double (heavy) cream, or more if making a softer ganache
450g/1lb plain (bittersweet) chocolate, at least 70 per cent cocoa solids, broken into pieces, or good-quality white chocolate, broken into pieces

METHOD
Gently heat the cream in a saucepan, but don't let it boil. Put either of the chocolates into a large heatproof bowl, pour over the hot cream (you will need only two-thirds if using white chocolate), stir once and let it stand for a few minutes to soften, then stir until completely melted (you might think it won't combine, but it will). When at room temperature, the ganache should ideally be spreadable like margarine. It will keep in the fridge for 2 weeks or can be cut into portion-sized cubes and frozen until needed. (Bring it back to room temperature before use.)

Whipped cream

MAKES ENOUGH FOR 1 SHAKE

125ml/4fl oz/½ cup double (heavy) cream

METHOD
Pour the cream into a large mixing bowl (less chance of getting it everywhere), then, using an electric or, if you fancy a work out, a balloon whisk, whisk to stiff peaks.

✿ If you don't think your freakshake is sweet enough (rare) or want the cream to hold up for longer, add 2 tablespoons icing (confectioners') sugar before whisking the cream. Avoid over-whisking as the cream will split and eventually end up as butter.

✿ Flavour or colour the cream with natural food flavouring or colouring, a little brandy or whisky, jam, vanilla extract, or sauces such as chocolate, raspberry, toffee or honey. It's normally best to add these before whisking, but again don't use too much. Avoid using lots of citrus or acidic liquids, as these will split the cream unless you're very careful.

FREAKSHAKES

Vanilla custard shake

MAKES 1 LARGE SHAKE

Glass Dressing
3–5 tbsp White Chocolate
  Ganache (page 12)
Toffee Popcorn (page 75)
shaved white chocolate
candy-coated sweets
Vanilla Fudge, crumbled (page
  56)

Shake
3 good scoops Vanilla Custard
  Ice Cream (page 10)
2 tbsp Vanilla Custard Sauce
  (page 77)
125ml/4fl oz/½ cup cold milk

Top Dressing
Whipped Cream, flavoured
  with a few drops of vanilla
  extract (page 12)
Meringue Kisses (page 55)
Baked Doughnut, filled with
  custard (page 58)
Toffee Popcorn (page 75)
Vanilla Custard Sauce, about
  1 tbsp (page 77)
icing (confectioners') sugar,
  for dusting

This rich and indulgent shake is a great starting point, especially if you want to keep things simple. Alternatively, I've added lots of ideas for top dressings for a more over-the-top shake.

BUILD
Lightly brush the inside of your glass and generously coat the rim with the ganache, then, throwing caution to the wind, stick the other dressing ingredients on top.

Put the ice cream, vanilla sauce and milk into a blender and lightly blend until thick and creamy. Pour the milkshake into the prepared glass.

Spoon or pipe the whipped vanilla cream over the shake in a conical shape. Decorate, starting with the meringue and doughnut then the popcorn and plenty of vanilla sauce. Finally, add a dusting of sugar, a spoon and a straw, and you're good to go...

Strawberry blush

MAKES 1 LARGE SHAKE

Glass Dressing
3–5 tbsp White Chocolate
  Ganache (page 12)
mini White Chocolate Drops,
  coloured pink (page 74)
Marshmallow, cut into mini
  mallows, coloured red and
  white (page 52)
Sugar-coated Popcorn
  (coloured pink) (page 75)
pink 100s & 1000s

Shake
3 good scoops Vanilla Custard
  Ice Cream (page 10)
3 tbsp good-quality strawberry
  jam (jelly)
4–6 frozen strawberries
125ml/4fl oz/½ cup cold milk

Top Dressing
Whipped Cream (page 12)
Shortbread, cut into squares
  (page 71)
White Chocolate Run-out,
  piped into a fan shape
  (page 74)
mini Jammie Dodger
  (optional)
Sugar-coated Popcorn,
  coloured pink (page 75)
Red Velvet Cookie (page 63)
Strawberry Sauce (page 77)

My wife's favourite, especially with a splash of Pimm's. It's a real taste of summer and would make a great addition to a Wimbledon tennis-watching party.

BUILD
Lightly brush the inside of your glass and generously coat the rim with the ganache, then randomly stick the other dressing ingredients on top.

Put the ice cream, jam, strawberries and milk into a blender and lightly blend until thick and creamy. Pour the milkshake into the prepared glass.

Spoon or pipe the whipped cream over the shake in a conical shape. Insert a straw and get artistic, adding the top dressing sweet treats, then finish with a drizzle of strawberry sauce.

Basic banana custard

MAKES 1 LARGE SHAKE

Glass Dressing
100g/3½oz/¾ cup flaked
    (slivered) almonds
few drops of banana
    flavouring (optional)
3–5 tbsp White Chocolate
    Ganache (page 12)
desiccated (dried shredded)
    coconut (toasted, optional)
Popping Corn (page 75)

Shake
3 good scoops Vanilla Custard
    Ice Cream (page 10)
1 ripe banana, peeled
125ml/4fl oz/½ cup cold milk

Top Dressing
Whipped Cream (page 12)
1 firm banana, peeled
Snickerdoodle Cookie (page
    65)
Vanilla Fudge, crumbled (page
    56)

A step up in the evolutionary chain, this is simply a flavoured vanilla custard shake. You can use other fruit, but avoid citrus as this can cause the milk and ice cream to curdle.

BUILD
Preheat the oven to 160°C/140°C fan/325°F/Gas 3. Line a baking sheet with baking paper, scatter over the almonds and toast for 8–10 minutes until they start to colour. Remove from the baking sheet and leave to cool before use. Store in an airtight container.

Stir a few drops of the banana flavouring, if using, into the ganache. Lightly brush the inside of your glass and generously coat the rim with the ganache. Put some coconut in the palm of one hand and roll the rim of the glass into it until lightly coated, then dot the ganache with some of the toasted almonds and popcorn.

Put the ice cream, banana and milk into a blender and lightly blend until thick and creamy. Pour the milkshake into the prepared glass.

Spoon or pipe the whipped cream (reserving a little for decorating) over the shake in a conical shape.

Cut the firm banana at an acute angle, poke it into the cream and stand the cookie on its end supported by the cream. Scatter with crumbled fudge and extra toasted almonds. Straw, spoon and sparkler, anyone?

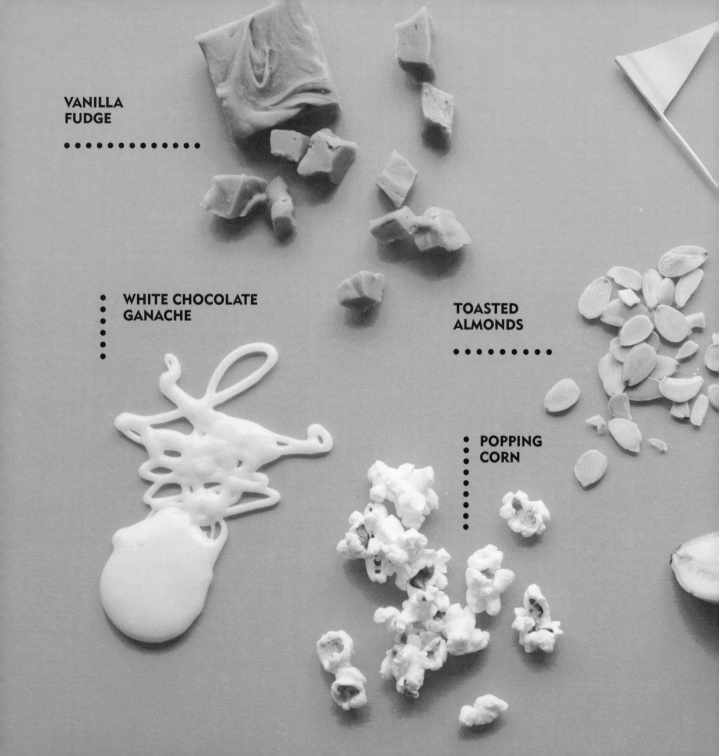

VANILLA FUDGE

WHITE CHOCOLATE GANACHE

TOASTED ALMONDS

POPPING CORN

DESICCATED
COCONUT

WHIPPED
CREAM

BANANA

SNICKERDOODLE
COOKIE

Double chocolate Oreo

MAKES 1 LARGE SHAKE

Glass Dressing
3 tbsp Plain Chocolate Ganache (page 12)
3 tbsp White Chocolate Ganache (page 12)
chopped nuts, of choice
Vanilla Fudge, crumbled (page 56)
Triple Chocolate Brownie, cut into small pieces (page 68)

Shake
3 good scoops Vanilla Custard Ice Cream (page 10)
3 Oreo cookies
3 tbsp Plain Chocolate Ganache, or to taste (page 12)
125ml/4fl oz/½ cup cold milk

Top Dressing
Whipped Cream (page 12)
Triple Chocolate Brownie (page 68)
Oreo cookie, Maltesers, chocolate flake
Marshmallows, toasted (page 52)
Chocolate Chip Cookie (page 62)
Baked Doughnut, filled with ganache (page 58)
Chocolate Sauce (page 77)

This is our most popular shake at Blue Dogs, closely followed by the Strawberry Berry Blush and Salted Caramel Banoffee Cream. Kids always gravitate towards chocolate, so we've started adding chocolate flavoured cream as well – it's a treat after all!

BUILD
Generously coat the rim of your glass with alternate dollops of white and plain chocolate ganache; I like to smear a little on the inside of the glass as well. Put the nuts and fudge in the palm of one hand and carefully dip the glass into the mixture to coat the rim. Stick a few pieces of brownie to the rim, too.

Put the ice cream, Oreos, ganache and milk into a blender and lightly blend until thick and creamy – you could leave some chunks of Oreo, if you like. Pour the milkshake into the prepared glass.

Spoon or pipe the whipped cream (reserving a little for decorating) over the shake in a conical shape.

Now, using your creativity, add a straw and your top dressing treats; start with the larger items, embedding them into the whipped cream, then add the smaller items and finally the chocolate sauce. Mmm… chocolate heaven.

CHOPPED
NUTS

TRIPLE
CHOCOLATE
BROWNIE

WHIPPED
CREAM

BAKED
DOUGHNUT

OREO
COOKIE

MALTESERS

CHOCOLATE
CHIP COOKIE

CHOCOLATE
SAUCE

TOASTED
MARSHMALLOWS

CHOCOLATE
FLAKE

Peanut butter brittle

MAKES 1 LARGE SHAKE

Glass Dressing
1 tbsp smooth or crunchy
    peanut butter
3–5 tbsp White Chocolate
    Ganache (page 12)
M&Ms
salted peanuts
jellybeans

Shake
3 good scoops Vanilla Custard
    Ice Cream (page 10)
2 tbsp peanut butter (more, if
    you like)
125ml/4fl oz/½ cup cold milk

Top Dressing
Whipped Cream (page 12)
Honeycomb, broken into
    chunks (page 51)
Peanut Brittle, broken into
    shards (page 57)
Peanut Butter Cookie (page
    64)
Marshmallows (page 52)
    (toasted, optional)
jellybeans
Toffee Sauce (page 76)

A nut lover's treat... although the brittle is made with peanuts
you could use any favourite nut. The nut butter gives the shake
a silky-smooth texture, or you could go chunky, if preferred.

BUILD

Add the peanut butter to the ganache and spread generously
over the rim of your glass. Casually spike the rim with the other
glass dressings.

Put the ice cream, peanut butter (adding more, if you like) and
milk into a blender and lightly blend until thick and creamy.
Pour or spoon the milkshake into the prepared glass.

Spoon or pipe the whipped cream (reserving a little for
decorating) over the shake in a conical shape.

Top with the sweet treats and lashings of toffee sauce, then
insert a super-thick straw (you'll need it as it's a thick shake)
and suck away...

Coffee mocha cracker

MAKES 1 LARGE SHAKE

Glass Dressing
few drops of coffee flavouring
3 tbsp White Chocolate
   Ganache (page 12)
3 tbsp Plain Chocolate
   Ganache (page 12)
Chocolate Coffee Beans (page
   74)
Vanilla Fudge, crumbled
   (page 56)
Sugar-Coated Popcorn (page
   27)

Shake
3 good scoops Vanilla Custard
   Ice Cream (page 10)
2–3 tbsp double-shot
   espresso, cooled, to taste
1 tbsp Plain Chocolate
   Ganache (page 12)
5 tbsp cold milk
1–2 shots Irish Cream
   (optional)

Top Dressing
Whipped Cream (page 12)
Easy Nutella Brownie (page
   68)
Chocolate Chip Cookie (page
   62)
Maltesers
Chocolate Sauce (page 77)
cocoa powder, for dusting

A grown-up freakshake made with a double shot of espresso, chocolate, cream and lots of treats. Why not add a shot of rum, whisky or brandy, instead of the Irish Cream, for extra indulgence?

BUILD
Stir the coffee flavouring into the white chocolate ganache. Generously coat the rim of your glass with alternate dollops of the coffee-flavoured ganache and plain chocolate ganache; a smear of each inside the glass adds an additional touch of finesse. You don't need a lot of dressing on this one; arrange just a few chocolate coffee beans, some fudge and popcorn for a more grown-up look.

Put the ice cream, cold espresso, ganache, milk and Irish Cream, if using, into a blender and lightly blend until thick and creamy. (If not using the Irish Cream, add another 2 tablespoons milk.) Pour the milkshake into the prepared glass.

Spoon or pipe the whipped cream (reserving a little for decorating) over the shake in a conical shape.

Top with a brownie, a small dollop of additional cream, then the cookie and a little more cream, next the Maltesers, chocolate sauce and a light dusting of cocoa powder. Slide in a straw between the brownie and the glass rim – sit back, relax and enjoy.

Salted caramel banoffee cream

MAKES 1 LARGE SHAKE

Glass Dressing
3 tbsp White Chocolate
 Ganache (page 12)
3 tbsp Plain Chocolate
 Ganache (page 12)
Toffee Popcorn (page 75)
Honeycomb, crumbled (page
 51)

Shake
3 good scoops Vanilla Custard
 Ice Cream (page 10)
2–3 tbsp Salted Caramel
 Sauce, to taste (page 76)
1 ripe banana, peeled
Marshmallows, about
 2.5cm/1in cube (page 52)
125ml/4fl oz/½ cup cold milk

Top Dressing
Whipped Cream (page 12)
sweet banana mallows
Vanilla Fudge, cut into chunks
 (page 56)
chocolate flake
Maltesers
salted pretzels
Salted Caramel Sauce (page
 76)

Banoffee pie in a glass and all the better for it! Go easy on the caramel sauce, if you don't like your shake too sweet; as I always say, feel free to mix and match your Freakshakes to suit your tastes.

BUILD
Generously coat the rim of your glass with alternate dollops of white and plain chocolate ganache. Casually spike the rim with the popcorn and honeycomb bits.

Put the ice cream, salted caramel sauce, banana, marshmallow (this thickens the shake and gives it a smooth, silky texture) and milk into a blender and lightly blend until thick and creamy. Pour the milkshake into the prepared glass.

Spoon or pipe the whipped cream over the shake in a conical shape.

Decorate generously with banana mallows, chunks of fudge, chocolate flake, Maltesers, salted pretzels, a straw and salted caramel sauce. Dive in...

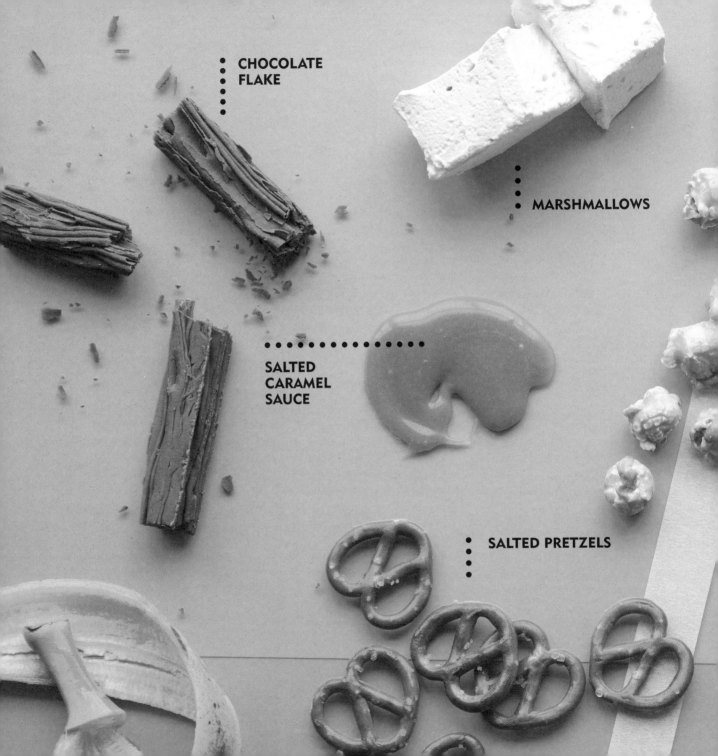

CHOCOLATE FLAKE

MARSHMALLOWS

SALTED CARAMEL SAUCE

SALTED PRETZELS

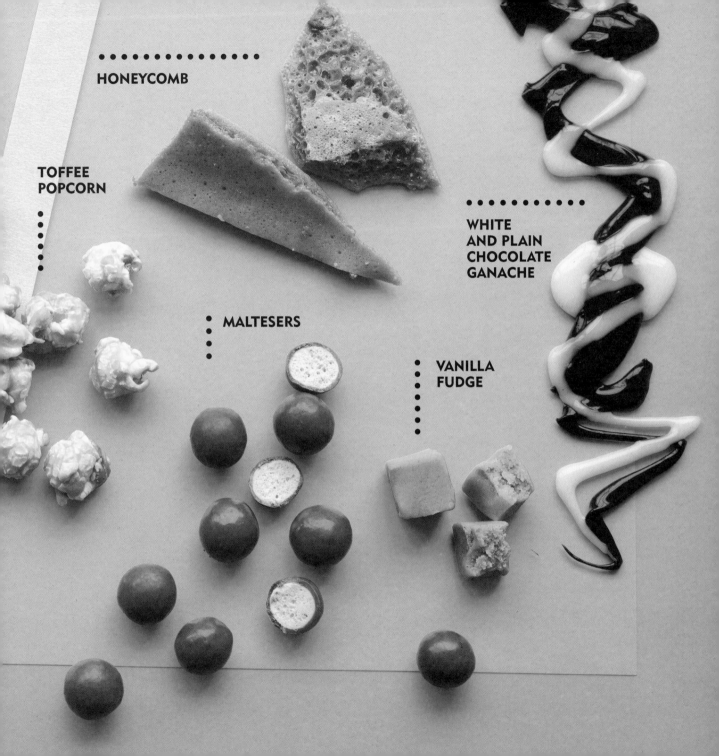

HONEYCOMB

TOFFEE
POPCORN

MALTESERS

WHITE
AND PLAIN
CHOCOLATE
GANACHE

VANILLA
FUDGE

Lemon meringue pie

MAKES 1 LARGE SHAKE

Glass Dressing
3–5 tbsp White Chocolate
    Ganache (page 12)
Marshmallows, cut into mini
    mallows (page 52)
Sugar-coated Popcorn (page
    75)
sugar strands

Shake
3 good scoops Vanilla Custard
    Ice Cream (page 10)
3 tbsp good-quality lemon
    curd
1 tbsp crumbled Shortbread
    (page 71), reserving a good
    pinch for decorating
Marshmallow, about
    2.5cm/1in cube (page 52)
125ml/4fl oz/½ cup cold milk

Top Dressing
Whipped Cream (page 12)
Vanilla Fudge, crumbled (page
    56)
Praline, broken into shards
    (page 57)
toasted almonds (page 18)
Chocolate Chip Cookie (page
    62)
Lemon Sauce (page 78)

My personal favourite… the fresh lemon curd really zings on the palate and the addition of marshmallow in the shake gives a velvety smooth texture. It really is lemon meringue pie in a glass!

BUILD

Lightly brush the inside of your glass and generously coat the rim with the ganache, then randomly stick the other dressing ingredients on top.

Put the ice cream, lemon curd, shortbread crumbs (reserving a good pinch to decorate), marshmallow and milk into a blender and lightly blend until thick and creamy. Pour the milkshake into the prepared glass.

Spoon or pipe the whipped cream (reserving a little for decorating) over the shake in a conical shape.

Now add the toppings, along with the reserved shortbread crumbs. Add a thick straw and drizzle over the lemon sauce.

SHORTBREAD

PRALINE
SHARD

CHOCOLATE
CHIP
COOKIES

LEMON CURD

TOASTED ALMONDS

MINI MARSHMALLOWS

SUGAR-COATED POPCORN

VANILLA FUDGE

MARSHMALLOWS

Mint chocolate hulk

MAKES 1 LARGE SHAKE

Glass Dressing
few drops of green colouring
3–5 tbsp White Chocolate
    Ganache (page 12)
chocolate flake, crumbled
jellybeans
Marshmallow, cut into mini
    mallows (page 52)

Shake
large handful of fresh mint
    leaves
2 tbsp caster (superfine) sugar
125ml/4fl oz/½ cup cold milk
3 good scoops Vanilla Custard
    Ice Cream (page 10)
1 shot spirit, try bourbon for
    a silky smooth Mint Julep
    (optional)

Top Dressing
Whipped Cream (page 12)
Mint Chocolate Bark (page
    48)
Marshmallows (page 52)
Honeycomb (page 51)
Maltesers
Chocolate Sauce (page 77)
fresh mint leaves
icing (confectioners') sugar,
    for dusting

Fresh mint really makes all the difference, here, but be aware that the herb loses its vibrant minty-green colour quite quickly. If you don't have fresh mint, replace it with a few drops of peppermint essence and a little green food colouring, but fresh is best.

BUILD
First start making the shake, put the fresh mint leaves, sugar and a little of the milk in a blender and blend to a fine paste. Set to one side while you dress the glass.

Swirl a few drops of green colouring into the ganache to give a marbled effect and then spread a generous layer around the rim of your glass. Crumble the chocolate flake into the palm of one hand and dip in the rim of the glass until coated, then top with jellybeans and mini mallows.

Put the ice cream, remaining milk, mint paste and your choice of spirit (if serving to adults, if not add a splash more milk) into a blender and lightly blend until thick and creamy. Pour the milkshake into the prepared glass.

Spoon or pipe the whipped cream over the shake in a conical shape.

Add the top dressing, starting with the larger pieces and then filling the gaps with the smaller treats. Add a straw, a drizzling of chocolate sauce, a couple of mint leaves and a dusting of icing sugar, then serve straightaway.

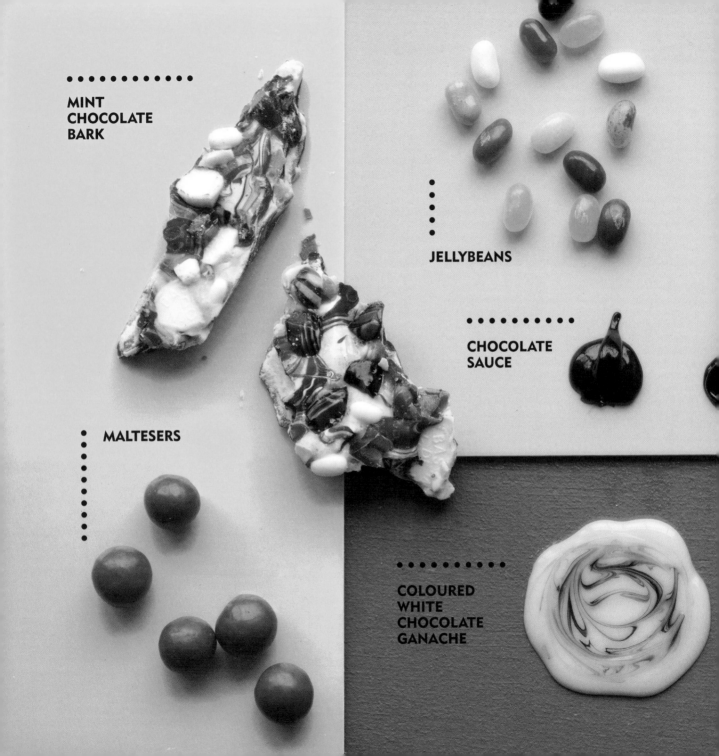

**MINT
CHOCOLATE
BARK**

JELLYBEANS

**CHOCOLATE
SAUCE**

MALTESERS

**COLOURED
WHITE
CHOCOLATE
GANACHE**

CHOCOLATE
FLAKE

FRESH MINT

HONEYCOMB

MARSHMALLOWS

Tropical coconut passion

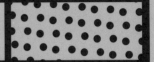

MAKES 1 LARGE SHAKE

Glass Dressing
3–5 tbsp White or Plain
Chocolate Ganache (page
12)
desiccated (dried shredded)
coconut

Shake
50g/1¾oz fresh or canned
pineapple pieces (drained
weight)
3 good scoops Vanilla Custard
Ice Cream (page 10)
2 tbsp coconut butter
1 ripe banana, peeled
125ml/4fl oz/½ cup cold milk
1 passion fruit, halved and/or
1 shot white rum

Top Dressing
Whipped Cream (page 12)
Marshmallows (page 52)
fruit jellies
Cranberry & Pistachio Bark
(page 48)

If you enjoy a smoothie or a Caribbean cocktail, then this is
for you. It really is worth adding the passion fruit as its slight
sharpness complements the sweetness of the shake beautifully,
and a shot of white rum works a treat, too.

BUILD
Generously coat the rim of your glass with the ganache. Put the
coconut in the palm of one hand and dip the rim of the glass
into it until lightly coated.

For the shake, if you're using fresh pineapple it's a good idea
to blend it for a few seconds before adding the rest of the
ingredients to give a smoother texture. Once blended, add
the ice cream, coconut butter, banana and milk and lightly
blend until thick and creamy. (If using canned pineapple, just
put everything in the blender together.) Stir in the passion fruit
(blending it breaks up the seeds and makes the shake gritty) and
the rum, if using. Pour the milkshake into the prepared glass.

Spoon or pipe the whipped cream over the shake in a conical
shape.

Decorate with the toppings, insert a thick straw and finish with
a big wedge of cranberry and pistachio bark.

Chocolate rum & raisin

MAKES 1 LARGE SHAKE

Glass Dressing
2 tbsp raisins
2 tbsp dark rum
3–5 tbsp Plain Chocolate
  Ganache (page 12)
desiccated (dried shredded)
  coconut
toasted almonds (page 18)
M&Ms

Shake
3 good scoops Vanilla Custard
  Ice Cream (page 10)
50g/1¾oz Nut & Raisin
  Chocolate Rum Relish
  (page 76)
2 tbsp Plain Chocolate
  Ganache (page 12)
2 tbsp peanut butter
125ml/4fl oz/½ cup cold milk

Top Dressing
Whipped Cream (page 12)
Cranberry & Pistachio Bark
  (page 48)
Marshmallows, toasted (page
  52)
Praline (page 57)
Vanilla Fudge (page 56)
Popping Corn (page 75)
Chocolate Sauce (page 77)

One for the adults… this shake with its rum-soaked raisins is a winner in our house, a real party favourite.

BUILD

This shake requires a little forward planning: soak the raisins in the rum and 1 tablespoon warm water for at least 1 hour or overnight, if time allows.

Generously coat the rim of your glass with the ganache. Put some coconut in the palm of one hand and dip the rim of the glass into it until lightly coated, then top with half of the drained soaked raisins, almonds and M&Ms.

Put the ice cream, nut and raisin relish, the remaining rum-soaked raisins (and any rum), ganache, peanut butter and milk into the blender and lightly blend until thick and creamy. Pour the milkshake into the prepared glass.

Spoon or pipe the whipped cream over the shake in a conical shape. Decorate with the top dressings and a generous amount of chocolate sauce.

Cherry cheesecake

MAKES 1 LARGE SHAKE

Glass Dressing
½ tsp beetroot (beet) powder
   or few drops of red food
   colouring
3–5 tbsp White Chocolate
   Ganache (page 12)
grated white chocolate
Marshmallow, cut into mini
   mallows (page 52)

Shake
3 good scoops Vanilla Custard
   Ice Cream (page 10)
100g/3½oz/⅔ cup fresh/
   frozen/canned drained
   pitted dark cherries (you
   can reserve the liquid from
   canned cherries to make the
   sauce)
1 medium slice Vanilla
   Cheesecake, cut into pieces
   (page 70)
125ml/4fl oz/½ cup cold milk
a splash of kirsch (optional)

Top Dressing
Whipped Cream (page 12)
toasted almonds (page 18)
Shortbread, crumbled (page
   71)
Cherry Sauce (page 78)
glazed cherry with stalk

Fresh cherries taste best when ripe and at the height of their season, but you can use frozen dark cherries at other times of the year. This is another of my wife Sarah's favourites and it just beat autumn apple pie freakshake into the book by a hair's breadth, maybe next time…

BUILD
Lightly stir the beetroot powder into the ganache to give a marbled effect. Generously coat the rim of your glass with the marbled ganache. Put the grated white chocolate in the palm of one hand and dip the glass into the chocolate to coat the rim, and then stud it with mini marshmallows.

Put the ice cream, cherries, cheesecake, milk and a splash of kirsch, if using, into a blender and lightly blend until thick and creamy. Pour the milkshake into the prepared glass.

Spoon or pipe the whipped cream (reserving a little for decorating) over the shake in a conical shape.

Top with the almonds, shortbread, cherry sauce and a glazed cherry. Add a straw and enjoy!

✿ **No worries, if you don't have a slice of cheesecake: try 50g/1¾oz/¼ cup cream cheese or mascarpone, 5 drops vanilla extract and 1 tablespoon icing (confectioners') sugar instead. Add them to the blender with 1 crumbled Shortbread (page 71) to give the texture of the cheesecake base.**

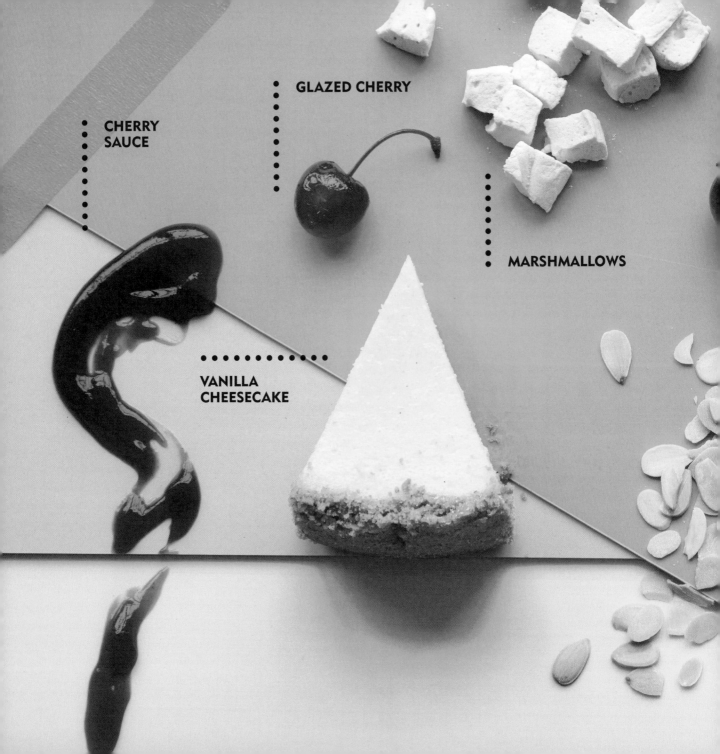

CHERRY
SAUCE

GLAZED CHERRY

MARSHMALLOWS

VANILLA
CHEESECAKE

WHITE CHOCOLATE
GANACHE

SHORTBREAD

TOASTED ALMONDS

DESICCATED COCONUT

BIG EXTRAS

Cranberry & pistachio bark

MAKES ABOUT 400G/14OZ

225g/8oz plain (bittersweet) chocolate, broken into
   pieces
3 tbsp honey
115g/4oz white chocolate, broken into pieces
4 tbsp dried cranberries
40g/1½oz/¼ cup shelled unsalted pistachio nuts
pinch of sea salt flakes

METHOD

Line a large baking tray with baking paper.

Put the plain chocolate in a heatproof bowl
set over a pan of simmering water; don't let
the bottom of the bowl touch the water. Melt
the chocolate, stirring occasionally. Stir in the
honey and set aside.

Melt the white chocolate following the
instructions, above.

Pour the plain chocolate mixture into the
prepared tray and spread out evenly. Drizzle
the melted white chocolate randomly
over the top. Scatter the cranberries and
pistachios over and sprinkle with sea salt. Tap
the tray on the counter to set the toppings
into the chocolate. Refrigerate until set and
then cut or break into pieces or shards.

Mint chocolate bark

MAKES ABOUT 1KG/2LB 4OZ

350g/12oz white chocolate, broken into pieces
1 tsp peppermint essence
2 tbsp vegetable oil
few drops of green food colouring
350g/12oz plain (bittersweet) chocolate, broken into
   pieces
225g/8oz mint candies, chopped or crushed

METHOD

Line a large baking tray with baking paper.

Melt the white chocolate following the
instructions, left. Add the peppermint
essence and half the vegetable oil; halve
the mixture. Add a few drops of green food
colouring to one half stirring to a smooth
even green colour. Set both aside.

Melt the plain chocolate as left, and stir in
the remaining oil.

Spoon the three different chocolate mixes
randomly into the prepared tray and spread
out evenly. Lightly mix them with the handle
of a wooden spoon to give a swirly, marbled
effect then scatter the mints over. Tap the
tray on the counter and refrigerate until set.

Honeycomb

MAKES ABOUT 250G/9OZ

unsalted butter, for greasing
200g/7oz/rounded 1 cup caster (superfine) sugar
5 tbsp golden (light corn) syrup
2 tsp bicarbonate of soda (baking soda)

METHOD

Grease and line a 20cm/8in square cake tin with baking paper. Put the sugar and syrup in a heavy-based saucepan over a gentle heat, stirring until the sugar has dissolved. Turn up the heat a little and let the mixture bubble until it turns a golden caramel colour; do not stir and keep your eyes on the mixture as it can easily burn.

Turn the heat off and, using a wooden spoon, stir in the bicarbonate of soda; take care as the sugar mixture can spit and foam up. Carefully, pour the mixture into the prepared tin. Leave to cool for about 1 hour until firm, then break into pieces.

Rocky road bark

MAKES ABOUT 400G/14OZ

350g/12oz white chocolate, broken into pieces
25g/1oz Marshmallow, cut into mini marshmallows (page 52)
85g/3oz M&Ms
85g/3oz glacé cherries, chopped
4 tbsp raisins

METHOD

Line a large baking tray with baking paper.

Melt the white chocolate following the method on page 48.

Pour the melted chocolate into the prepared tray and spread out evenly. Scatter mini marshmallows, M&Ms, glacé cherries and raisins randomly over the top.

Tap the tray on the counter a couple of times to set the toppings into the chocolate. Refrigerate until set and then cut or break into pieces or shards.

Store in an airtight container in the fridge or freezer until ready to use.

Marshmallow

**MAKES 40–80,
DEPENDING ON SIZE**

2 tbsp powdered gelatine
sunflower oil, for greasing
85g/3oz/¾ cup icing
   (confectioners') sugar, for
   dusting
225g/8oz/heaped 1 cup
   granulated sugar
125ml/4fl oz/½ cup golden
   syrup (divided in two)
pinch of salt
few drops of food colouring
   (optional)
1 tsp vanilla extract

✱ **To toast
marshmallows, impale
your marshmallow on
a fork or skewer then
lightly toast, either in
the flame of your gas
hob (stove) or using a
blowtorch; take care
as the marshmallow
becomes very hot.**

METHOD

Sprinkle the gelatine over 4 tablespoons warm water in a small bowl and leave to soften for 5–10 minutes before draining.

Lightly grease a 30 x 16cm/12 x 6¼in tray bake tin (you could use a smaller tin for deeper marshmallows) and liberally dust with some of the icing sugar to coat the bottom and sides.

Mix together the sugar, half the golden syrup, salt, food colouring, if using, and 125ml/4fl oz/½ cup water in a medium saucepan over a high heat. Bring to the boil for 10–15 minutes; stop when the temperature on a sugar thermometer is 120°C/248°F.

While the mixture is boiling, pour the remaining golden syrup and the softened gelatine into the bowl of an electric mixer fitted with a whisk. Set the mixer speed to low and when the sugar mixture has reached the correct temperature, pour it into the mixer bowl. Increase the speed to medium and beat for 6–7 minutes until very thick, white and fluffy, then beat in the vanilla extract.

Pour the mixture into the prepared tin, smoothing it into the corners with a palette knife. Sift icing sugar evenly and generously over the top and leave to set for at least 4 hours in a cool, dry place.

Use a knife to loosen the marshmallow from the edges of the tin and turn out onto an icing sugar-dusted work surface. Cut into pieces (a pizza cutter works well) or shapes with cutters. Dip the sticky cut edges in more icing sugar and shake off any excess.

Meringue kisses

MAKES ABOUT 36, DEPENDING ON SIZE

300g/10½oz/rounded 1½ cups caster (superfine) sugar
150g/5½oz egg whites, at room temperature

METHOD

Preheat the oven to 100°C/80°C fan/225°F/Gas¼. Line a baking tray with baking paper, scatter the sugar over and warm in the oven for 10 minutes.

Put the egg whites in a large, grease-free mixing bowl and whisk on high until they form stiff peaks. Whisking continuously, add the warmed sugar, a large spoonful at a time, until a smooth and shiny; ensure the mixture returns to the peak stage between each addition of sugar.

Spoon the mixture into a piping (pastry) bag, with or without food colouring (see below), and pipe into 1cm/½in small meringues on the prepared baking tray. Bake for 30–40 minutes until crisp on the outside but still soft in the middle, then turn off the oven and leave the meringues to cool in the oven with the door ajar. Remove from the tray and store in an airtight container.

✽ Colour/flavour the meringue by turning the piping bag inside out before filling, then spread your choice of colour/flavour in stripes down the length of the bag. Turn the bag the right way round, spoon in the meringue mixture and pipe as required.

Vanilla fudge

MAKES ABOUT
1KG/2LB 4OZ

sunflower oil, for greasing
250g/9oz/2¼ sticks unsalted
    butter, at room temperature
397g/14oz can condensed
    milk
175ml/6fl oz/⅔ cup milk
2 tbsp golden (light corn)
    syrup
800g/1lb 12oz/4 cups
    granulated sugar
2 tsp vanilla extract

METHOD

Place a small bowl of cold water next to your hob. Lightly grease a 30 x 20cm/12 x 8in, or 25cm/9in square cake tin and line with baking paper.

Put all the ingredients, except the vanilla extract, in a large heavy-based saucepan and bring to a gentle boil, stirring constantly. Stop stirring once the mixture comes to the boil and continue to boil gently for 12–20 minutes until the mixture turns golden. You need to achieve soft-ball stage on a sugar thermometer, about 118°C/235°F. Alternatively, using a fork, drop a little of the molten fudge into the bowl of water; it should turn into a soft pliable ball when pressed.

Turn off the heat and gently stir in the vanilla extract. Leave the mixture to cool until thickened; it is ready when the blunt edge of a knife leaves a visible line when dragged through the fudge. Beat the fudge until thickened to the texture of stiff peanut butter with an electric whisk or wooden spoon.

Pour the fudge into the prepared tin and smooth the top. You can cool the fudge in the fridge, but for no longer than 2 hours or it will set too hard. When firm, cut the fudge into squares and store in an airtight container in a cool, dry place.

Praline

**MAKES ABOUT
350G/12OZ**

200g/7oz/1 cup granulated
   sugar
150g/5½oz/heaped 1 cup
   mixed unsalted nuts
good pinch of sea salt
   (optional)

✿ To make peanut
brittle, replace the
mixed nuts with
unsalted peanuts.

METHOD

Line a baking tray with silicon paper. Put 3 tablespoons water
into a heavy-based frying pan or skillet over a medium heat and
bring to the boil. Add the sugar and stir until it has dissolved.

Turn the heat up and cook until the sugar has caramelized,
about 150°C/300°F on a sugar thermometer (hard-crack stage);
you can gently swirl the pan occasionally to obtain an evenly
coloured syrup, but don't stir it.

Reduce the heat and add the nuts, stir once to coat the nuts in
the syrup, then pour the hot mixture onto the prepared baking
tray in an even layer. Sprinkle all over with sea salt and leave to
cool until set.

Peel the praline off the paper and break into pieces.

Baked doughnuts

MAKES ABOUT 24

275ml/9½fl oz/generous
1 cup full-fat milk
50g/1¾oz/3½ tbsp unsalted
butter
500g/1lb 2oz/3¾ cups plain
(all-purpose) flour, sifted,
plus extra for dusting
1 tsp instant (fast-action) dried
yeast
½ tsp salt
75g/2¾oz/heaped ⅓ cup
caster (superfine) sugar
1 free-range egg, beaten

To finish
100g/3½oz/7 tbsp unsalted
butter, melted
100g/3½oz/½ cup caster
(superfine) sugar
350g/12oz/3⅓ cups good-
quality strawberry jam (jelly)
(optional), or other filling
(see below)

♣ You can use any
flavour of jam, or
custard, lemon curd or
chocolate ganache to
fill the doughnuts.

METHOD

Line a baking sheet with baking paper. Bring the milk to the boil in a heavy-based saucepan, remove from the heat and stir in the butter until melted. Leave to cool to 37°C/98°F.

Mix together the flour, yeast, salt and sugar in a large mixing bowl, or use a mixer with a dough hook. Stir in the egg and the milk mixture.

Tip the dough out onto a lightly floured surface and knead for 10 minutes (or use your mixer). Put the dough in a clean bowl, cover and leave in a warm place until doubled in size, about 2 hours. Lightly knock back the dough, kneading it briefly on a lightly floured surface, or giving it a short burst in the mixer.

Divide the dough into 24 equal pieces and roll each one into a ball. Place them, spaced well apart, on the prepared baking sheet and leave covered in a warm place until almost doubled in size.

Preheat the oven to 180°C/160°C fan/350°F/Gas 4. Place a roasting tin three-quarters full of hot water in the bottom of the oven. Bake the doughnuts for 12–15 minutes until golden brown. Remove from the oven, leave to cool for 10 minutes then brush with melted butter and roll in sugar and serve warm.

If filling your doughnuts with jam, spoon it into a piping bag fitted with a pointed nozzle, then pierce each doughnut with the nozzle and squeeze a little jam into the middle.

COOKIES

Chocolate chip cookies

115g/4oz/1 stick softened
  unsalted butter
130g/4¾oz/¾ cup light soft
  brown sugar
85g/3oz/⅓ cup granulated
  sugar
1 large (US extra-large)
  free-range egg, at room
  temperature
½ tsp vanilla extract
200g/7oz/1½ cups plain (all-
  purpose) flour, sifted
1 tsp bicarbonate of soda
  (baking soda)
2 tsp cornflour (cornstarch)
2 tsp salt
300g/10½oz/2 cups
  chocolate chips

✿ Stuff or spike
the dough with
M&Ms, chunks of
Turkish Delight and
Marshmallows (page
52) instead of the
chocolate chips before
baking.

METHOD

Preheat the oven to 180°C/160°C fan/350°F/Gas 4 and line a baking sheet with baking paper. In a large mixing bowl, cream the butter and both types of sugar with an electric whisk until light and creamy, then beat in the egg and vanilla extract.

In a separate large bowl, mix all the dry ingredients together.

Slowly add the wet ingredients to the dry to form a dough and refrigerate for 1 hour to firm up.

Roll the dough into a sausage shape, about 3cm/1¼in diameter, using clingfilm (plastic wrap) to help, then slice into 2cm/¾in thick discs. (The uncooked cookies can be frozen at this point, but thaw before baking.) Place the cookies, spaced well apart, on the prepared baking sheet and bake for 10–12 minutes until light golden around the edges.

Remove from the oven and leave to cool for 10 minutes on the baking sheet, then place on a wire rack to cool completely.

Red velvet cookies

MAKES ABOUT 10

200g/7oz/1½ cups plain
   (all-purpose) flour, sifted
20g/¾oz/1/4 cup cocoa
   powder
1 tsp bicarbonate of soda
   (baking soda)
¼ tsp salt
115g/4oz/1 stick softened
   unsalted butter
150g/5½oz/¾ cup light or
   dark soft brown sugar
50g/1¾oz/¼ cup
   granulated sugar
1 free-range egg, at room
   temperature
1 tbsp milk
2 tsp vanilla extract
2 tsp beetroot (beet) powder
   or 1½ tsp red food colouring
175g/6oz/1 heaped cup white
   or milk chocolate chips
icing (confectioners') sugar,
   for dusting

METHOD

Preheat the oven to 180°C/160°C fan/350°F/Gas 4 and line a
baking sheet with baking paper. Sift the flour, cocoa powder,
bicarbonate of soda and salt into a mixing bowl and set aside.

In a separate large mixing bowl, beat the butter for about 1
minute until creamed. Add both types of sugar and beat on a
medium speed until combined. Beat in the egg, milk, vanilla
extract and beetroot powder or food colouring. Fold in the dry
ingredients and chocolate chips to make a dough. Refrigerate for
at least 1 hour.

Divide the dough into 75g/2¾oz balls. Place on the prepared
baking sheet, spaced well apart, and bake for 11–13 minutes or
until light golden around the edges. Remove from the oven and
press down lightly on each one to form the trademark cracks.
Leave to cool on a wire rack then lightly dust with icing sugar.

Peanut butter cookies

MAKES ABOUT 5

60g/2¼oz/4 tbsp peanut
  butter
30g/1oz/2 tbsp softened
  unsalted butter
100g/3½oz/½ cup light soft
  brown sugar
½ tsp vanilla extract
1 free-range egg, at room
  temperature
100g/3½oz/¾ cup plain
  (all-purpose) flour, sifted
½ tsp bicarbonate of soda
  (baking soda)
2 tbsp granulated sugar, for
  coating

METHOD

Preheat the oven to 180°C/160°C fan/350°F/Gas 4 and line a
baking sheet with baking paper. In a large mixing bowl, beat
together the peanut butter, butter and brown sugar until smooth.
Add the vanilla extract and egg and beat until creamy.

Sift the flour and bicarbonate of soda into the bowl and slowly
fold into the wet ingredients to form a dough. Divide the dough
into 80g/2¾oz balls and roll them in the granulated sugar.

Place on the prepared baking sheet, spaced well apart, flatten
the tops slightly and bake for 12 minutes or until light golden
around the edges. Remove from the oven and leave to cool for
10 minutes on the baking sheet, then place on a wire rack to
cool completely.

Snickerdoodle cookies

MAKES ABOUT 14

100g/3½oz/7 tbsp softened
  unsalted butter
160g/5¾oz/¾ cup granulated
  sugar, plus 85g/3oz/heaped
  ⅓ cup for coating
70g/2½oz/⅓ cup light soft
  brown sugar
1 large (US extra-large)
  free-range egg, at room
  temperature
1 tsp vanilla extract
200g/7oz/1½ cups plain (all-
  purpose) flour, sifted
½ tsp bicarbonate of soda
  (baking soda)
¼ tsp cream of tartar
¼ tsp salt (optional)
2 tsp ground cinnamon

METHOD

Preheat the oven to 180°C/160°C fan/350°F/Gas 4. Line a baking sheet with baking paper. In a large mixing bowl, cream the butter, the larger quantity of granulated sugar and the brown sugar with an electric whisk for about 3 minutes. Add the egg and vanilla extract and beat for another 3 minutes. Fold in the flour, bicarbonate of soda and salt (if using) to make a dough.

Divide the dough into 14 equal balls, flatten slightly, and refrigerate for at least 1 hour.

Mix together the remaining granulated sugar and the cinnamon on a plate. Roll each cookie into the mixture and place, spaced well apart, on the prepared baking sheet. Bake for 10 minutes until light golden around the edges. Remove from the oven and leave to cool on the baking sheet.

CAKES

Triple chocolate brownies

MAKES 9 SQUARES

225g/8oz plain (bittersweet) chocolate, broken into
    pieces
65g/2¾oz milk chocolate, broken into pieces
275g/9¾oz/2½ sticks unsalted butter, cut into pieces,
    plus extra for greasing
4 free-range eggs
400g/14oz/2⅓ cups caster (superfine) sugar
2 tbsp vanilla extract
175g/6oz/1½ cups plain (all-purpose) flour, sifted
250g/9oz white chocolate, broken into small pieces

METHOD
Preheat the oven to 180°C/160°C fan/350°F/
Gas 4. Line a 25cm/10in square brownie tin
with baking paper and grease the sides. Melt
both chocolates together with the butter in
a pan over a low heat. Set aside to cool.

Meanwhile, whisk the eggs, sugar and vanilla
in a large mixing bowl until light and creamy.
Stir in the melted chocolate mixture and fold
in the flour and white chocolate pieces.

Pour the brownie mixture into the prepared
tin, level the top and bake for 40–45 minutes
until the outer edges are cooked. Leave to cool
for 10 minutes before turning out onto a wire
rack to cool completely. Cut into squares.

Easy Nutella brownies

MAKES 9 SQUARES

unsalted butter, for greasing
3 free-range eggs
500g/1lb 2oz Nutella or other chocolate hazelnut
    spread
100g/3½oz/¾ cup plain (all-purpose) flour, sifted

METHOD
Preheat the oven to 180°C/160°C fan/350°F/
Gas 4. Line a 20cm/8in square brownie tin
with baking paper and grease the sides.
Whisk the eggs until pale, then beat in the
Nutella and fold in the flour.

Pour the brownie mixture into the prepared
tin, level the top and bake for 20 minutes
until the outer edges are cooked but the
middle is still squidgy. Leave to cool for 10
minutes before turning out onto a wire rack
to cool completely. Cut into 9 squares.

Flapjacks

MAKES 10 SLICES OR 36 SMALL CUBES

225g/8oz/2 sticks unsalted butter, plus extra for greasing
225g/8oz/rounded 1 cup light soft brown sugar
175g/6oz/⅔ cup golden (light corn) syrup
450g/1lb/4⅔ cups rolled oats

METHOD

Preheat the oven to 180°C/160°C fan/350°F/Gas 4. Line a 20cm/8in square cake tin with baking paper and grease the sides.

Melt the butter, sugar and golden syrup together until the sugar has dissolved. Stir in the oats and pour the mixture into the prepared tin. Bake for 30 minutes until firm. Remove from the oven, leave to cool to room temperature and cut into slices or cubes.

Vanilla cheesecake

MAKES ABOUT 10 SLICES

- 85g/3oz/5½ tbsp unsalted butter, melted, plus extra for greasing
- 14 digestive biscuits (Graham crackers) or other sweetmeal biscuits, crushed
- 550g/1lb 4oz/2½ cups cream cheese, at room temperature
- 200g/7oz/1 cup granulated sugar
- 2 tbsp cornflour (cornstarch)
- 3 large (US extra-large) free-range eggs
- 1 free-range egg yolk
- 3 tbsp double (heavy) cream
- 2 tsp vanilla extract
- 1 vanilla pod, split lengthways and seeds scraped out

METHOD

Preheat the oven to 200°C/180°C fan/400°F/Gas 6. Line a deep 20cm/8in cake tin (not a springform tin) with baking paper and grease the sides. To make the base, mix together the crushed biscuits and melted butter, then press the mixture into the base of the prepared tin in an even layer.

In a large mixing bowl, beat the cream cheese, sugar and cornflour with an electric whisk on a low speed until smooth. Add the eggs, one at a time, scraping down the bowl between each addition. Make sure each egg is thoroughly mixed in before adding the next to avoid the mixture splitting. Whisk in the egg yolk, cream and vanilla extract. Stir in the vanilla seeds (save the pods to make vanilla sugar, page 10). Pour the filling mixture over the base.

Put the cake tin into a large roasting pan then add enough just-boiled water from a kettle to come halfway up the side of the tin. Bake for 15 minutes, then turn the oven down to 150°C/130°C fan/300°F/Gas 2 and bake for another 1 hour–1¼ hours until the edge is set and the middle is still a bit wobbly. Turn off the oven, leave the door ajar, and let the cheesecake cool for 1 hour or so, then remove from the oven and leave to cool completely. Transfer to a serving plate and chill until ready to serve.

Shortbread

MAKES 10 SLICES OR 36 SQUARES

225g/8oz/2 sticks softened butter, plus extra for greasing
100g/3½oz/½ cup caster (superfine) sugar, plus extra for sprinkling
280g/10oz/1¾ cups plain (all-purpose) flour, sifted
¼ tsp baking powder
½ tsp salt

METHOD

Preheat the oven to 180°C/160°C fan/350°F/Gas 4. Line a 20cm/8in square cake tin with baking paper and grease the sides. Beat the softened butter with the sugar until light and creamy. Add the flour, baking powder and salt. Mix well and bring together the mixture into a ball with your hands; don't worry if it is a bit crumbly.

Tip the dough into the prepared tin and press down into an firm, even layer with your fingers. Score the dough with a knife into the required number of pieces and prick each piece with a fork. Bake for 20 minutes until light golden, remove from the oven and sprinkle with sugar. Leave to cool before removing from the tin then cut into pieces.

TOPPINGS

Chocolate drops

MAKES ABOUT 100G/3½OZ/⅔ CUP

100g/3½oz white, milk or plain (bittersweet)
   chocolate, broken into pieces

METHOD
Put the chocolate in a heatproof bowl set
over a pan of simmering water; don't let the
bottom of the bowl touch the water. Melt
the chocolate, stirring occasionally.

Line a baking sheet with baking paper. Drip
or pipe the melted chocolate into rounds.
Leave to cool and set, then peel the drops
away from the paper.

✽ **Try colouring the white chocolate drops
with natural food colouring; stir a few
drops into the melted chocolate.**

✽ **To make chocolate run-outs, melt your
choice of chocolate, as above. Pour the
melted chocolate into a piping (pastry)
bag with a very fine nozzle (tip). Line a
baking sheet with baking paper. Pipe the
chocolate into random squiggles, shapes
or into a lace effect. Leave to cool and set,
then peel the shapes away from the paper.**

Chocolate coffee beans

MAKES ABOUT 150G/5½OZ/⅔ CUP

100g/3½oz white, milk or plain (bittersweet) chocolate,
   broken into pieces
50g/1¾oz/¾ cup coffee beans

METHOD
Melt your choice of chocolate as left.

Stir in the coffee beans until well coated.

Line a baking sheet with silicon paper.

Lift the beans out of the melted chocolate
and arrange them on the prepared sheet,
leaving enough space between them so they
don't stick together.

Leave to cool and set, then peel the beans
off the paper. They can be stored in an
airtight container in a cool place.

Popping corn

MAKES ABOUT 100G/3½OZ/12 CUPS

25g/1oz/1½ tbsp unsalted butter
100g/3½oz/½ cup dried popcorn kernels
salt or icing (confectioners') sugar, to taste (optional)

METHOD
Melt the butter in a heavy-based saucepan with a tight-fitting lid over a medium heat. Add the corn kernels, replace the lid and, holding the lid in place, agitate the pan backwards and forwards.

After a minute or so you will hear the corn start to pop; don't be tempted to remove the lid until the popping stops. Once the popping has stopped, remove the lid and add a little salt or icing sugar, if desired.

✿ **For fun, add a few drops of food colouring to the butter before heating.**

Toffee popcorn
MAKES ABOUT 500G/1LB 2OZ/12 CUPS

115g/4oz/1 stick unsalted butter, plus extra for greasing
100g/3½oz/½ cup dried popcorn kernels
150g/5½oz/1¼ cups salted peanuts (optional)
250g/9oz/½ cups light soft brown sugar

5 tbsp golden (light corn) syrup
1 tsp vanilla extract
½ tsp bicarbonate of soda (baking soda)

METHOD
Preheat the oven to 120°C/100°C fan/250°F/Gas ½. Line a large baking sheet with baking paper and grease with butter.

Pop the corn following the instructions, left. Put the popped corn, taking out any unpopped kernels, into a large mixing bowl with the peanuts, if using.

Melt the butter, sugar and syrup in a heavy-based saucepan over a gentle heat until the sugar has dissolved, then bring to a rolling boil for about 3 minutes, stirring constantly. Remove from the heat, add the vanilla extract and bicarbonate of soda (the mixture will bubble up a little bit) and stir.

Pour the hot mixture over the popcorn and peanuts and gently stir until coated. Spread out evenly onto the prepared baking sheet, then bake for about 1 hour. Remove from the oven, leave to cool then break into pieces.

Syrups & sauces

Toffee sauce

MAKES ABOUT 500ML/17FL OZ/2 CUPS

300ml/10fl oz/1¼ cups double (heavy) cream
50g/1¾oz/3½ tbsp unsalted butter
175g/6oz/1¾ cups light soft brown sugar

METHOD
Put all the ingredients, except the salt, in a heavy-based saucepan. Set the pan over a low heat and stir until the sugar has dissolved. Turn the heat up and let the sauce bubble for 2–3 minutes until thickened and golden brown.

Leave to cool or refrigerate for up to 3 days and bring back to room temperature before use. (If the sauce is too thick or dark, stir in extra cream.) The sauce can also be gently reheated, if you like.

✿ **For a boozy sauce, add 2 tbsp rum, whisky, bourbon or Irish cream to the cooled toffee sauce.**

✿ **For a salted caramel sauce, add a good pinch or two of sea salt to the cooled toffee sauce.**

Nut & raisin chocolate rum relish

70g/2½oz/½ cup mixed dried fruit, such as raisins, sultanas (golden raisins), cherries or appricots
3 tbsp dark rum
70g/2½oz/½ cup mixed nuts, such as almonds, hazelnuts, pecans, walnuts, pistachios, brazil nuts, peanuts or cashews
70g/2½oz/½ cup plain (bittersweet) chocolate, broken into pieces

METHOD
First soak the mixed dried fruit in the dark rum for at least 1 hour or overnight, if time allows, until softened. Drain the fruit and reserve the rum.

Follow the instructions for the Toffee Sauce, left. Stir in the drained soaked dried fruit, the mixed nuts and plain chocolate. Stir until the chocolate melts, then leave to cool and stir in the reserved rum.

Strawberry sauce

MAKES ABOUT 200ML/7FL OZ/SCANT 1 CUP

100g/3½oz/rounded ½ cup caster (superfine) sugar
100g/3½oz/1 cup strawberries, hulled
1 tbsp arrowroot or cornflour (cornstarch)

METHOD
Put the sugar in a saucepan with 2 tablespoons water and heat gently, stirring, until the sugar has dissolved. Blend the strawberries, add them to the pan and bring to the boil.

Dissolve the arrowroot or cornflour in a little water. Add to the pan then reduce the heat slightly and simmer, stirring, until the sauce has thickened and coats the back of a spoon. Leave to cool and pass through a fine sieve (strainer) for a smooth sauce.

Chocolate sauce

MAKES ABOUT 200ML/7FL OZ/SCANT 1 CUP

100ml/3½fl oz/¾ cup double (heavy) cream
100g/3½oz good-quality plain (bittersweet), milk or
    white chocolate, broken into pieces
30g/1oz/2 tbsp unsalted butter
flavouring/colouring (optional)

METHOD
Gently warm the cream in a saucepan until hot. Put the chocolate and butter in a heatproof bowl, pour over the hot cream and stir until the chocolate has melted. Serve or add flavouring and/or colouring, if you like.

Vanilla custard sauce

MAKES ABOUT 550ML/19FL OZ/2¼ CUPS

400ml/14fl oz/1⅔ cups milk
1 tsp vanilla extract
70g/2½oz/scant ½ cup caster (superfine) sugar
3 free-range egg yolks

METHOD
Follow the instructions for making the Vanilla Custard Ice Cream (page 10), using milk and vanilla extract instead of cream and vanilla pods. Leave the sauce to cool before using.

Lemon sauce

MAKES ABOUT 250ML/9FL OZ/1 CUP

juice of 1 lemon
100g/3½oz/½ cup granulated sugar
30g/1oz/2 tbsp unsalted butter
good pinch of sea salt
¼ tsp nutmeg, to taste (optional)
1 tbsp cornflour (cornstarch)

METHOD
Put the lemon juice, sugar, butter, salt,
nutmeg, if using, and 225ml/8fl oz/scant
1 cup water in a saucepan and bring to
the boil.

Dissolve the cornflour in a little cold water.
Add to the pan then reduce the heat slightly
and simmer, stirring, until the sauce has
thickened and coats the back of a spoon.
Leave to cool and pass through a fine sieve
(strainer) for a smooth sauce.

Cherry sauce

**MAKES ABOUT 200ML/7FL OZ/SCANT
1 CUP**

100g/3½oz/⅔ cup fresh, canned (reserving 2 tbsp
   of the juice), or frozen pitted dark cherries (defrost
   before use)
100g/3½oz/½ cup caster (superfine) sugar
pinch of salt
pinch of ground cinnamon (optional)
1 tbsp arrowroot or cornflour (cornstarch)

METHOD
Put the cherries and sugar in a saucepan
with 2 tablespoons water (or juice from the
canned cherries) and bring to a gentle boil,
stirring, until the sugar has dissolved. Using
a hand blender, blend the cherry mixture
until smooth, stir in the salt and cinnamon,
then return to the boil.

Dissolve the arrowroot or cornflour
(cornstarch) in a little water. Add to the
pan then reduce the heat slightly and
simmer, stirring, until the sauce has
thickened and coats the back of a spoon.
Leave to cool and pass through a fine sieve
(strainer) for a smooth sauce.

First published in the United Kingdom
in 2017 by Pavilion

43 Great Ormond Street
London
WC1N 3HZ

ISBN 978-1-91121-675-9

A CIP catalogue record for this book is available from the
British Library.

10 9 8 7 6 5 4 3 2 1

Reproduction by Mission Productions Ltd, Hong Kong
Printed and bound by 1010 Printing International Ltd, China

This book can be ordered direct from the publisher at
www.pavilionbooks.com

Publisher's Acknowledgements
With thanks to photographer Clare Winfield and the rest of the
photography team, Valerie Berry, Alexander James Gray and
Charlie Phillips.